# Where does Electricity come from?

**Susan Mayes**
Designed by Mike Pringle
Illustrated by John Shackell and John Scorey

Revised by Philippa Wingate
Cover design by Russell Punter
Cover illustration by Christyan Fox
With thanks to Katarina Dragoslavić and Rosie Dickins
Series editor: Heather Amery

## CONTENTS

2 Electricity at work
4 Electricity and light
5 Electricity and heat
6 How a battery works
8 How a telephone works
9 About television
10 Electricity to your home
12 How electricity is made

14 Power from water
16 Going places
18 Other electricity
20 More power
22 Useful words
23 Internet links
24 Index

# Electricity at work

Electricity gives power, light and heat to cities, towns and villages all over the world.

Electricity makes street lights work and powers a high-speed train.

It can travel long distances to work in places far away.

*Internet link* For a link to a website with an interactive guide on electricity that gets you thinking about how electricity is used, go to **www.usborne-quicklinks.com**

You cannot see electricity but you can see where it is working around you, all the time.

How is electricity made? How does it get to your home and what can it do?

You can find out about all of these things in this book.

*Internet link* For a link to a website where you can see how electricity gets to your home, go to *www.usborne-quicklinks.com*

# Electricity and light

The first electric light bulb was made by Thomas Edison in 1879. Now millions of them are used all over the world.

How many light bulbs can you count in and around your home?

## Inside a light bulb

When you turn on a switch, electricity goes through the wires into the bulb.

It goes into a thin coil of wire, called a filament, and makes it heat up.

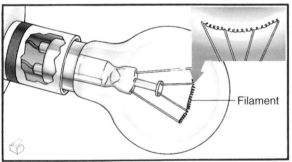

Filament

The filament is made of a metal called tungsten, which gets hot without melting.

It gets hotter and hotter until it glows white. This glow is the light you see.

### Did you know?

Some lighthouses use lamps which are 20 times brighter than bulbs in your home.

Special mirrors make the light shine as far as 40 kilometres (24 miles) over the sea.

4    **Electricity can be very dangerous. Never play with it.**

# Electricity and heat

Special wires which carry electricity heat up when the electricity flows through them.

Hot wires are very useful because they heat up all sorts of things.

An electric heater has heating wires inside. When electricity goes through them, they get hot and the heater warms the room.

Electricity heats coils of wire in a hairdryer. A fan blows air over the hot wires. This heats up the air so you can dry your hair.

On most electric cookers, each ring has a heating wire inside. The electricity flows through and heats the ring, so you can cook on it.

## Did you know?

Some football pitches have heating wires under the ground.

They stop the pitch from freezing when the weather is cold.

**Never use anything electrical near water.**

# How a battery works

Some toys need a small amount
of electricity to make them work.
They get it from a battery.

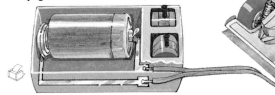

Inside the battery, special chemicals
work together to make the electricity.
It then travels through the wires

to make the toy work. The battery
stops working when the chemicals
are used up.

## Things which use batteries

Many watches use electricity from
tiny, thin batteries.

A torch bulb lights up when
electricity from the batteries
passes through it.

A car has a special, powerful
battery. Its electricity makes the
engine, lights and heater work.

*Internet link* For a link to a website where you can try an online experiment using batteries
and light bulbs, go to **www.usborne-quicklinks.com**

## Try this

To light up a bulb you will need:
– 2 pieces of flex (wire covered with plastic)
– a 1.5 volt torch battery
– a 1.5 volt torch bulb
– a bulb holder
– sticky tape
– a small screwdriver
– a pair of scissors

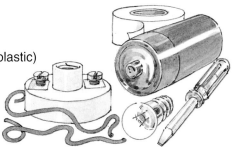

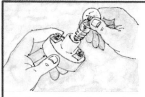

**1.** Screw the bulb into the bulb holder.

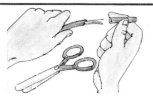

**2.** Strip off the plastic at each end of the wire.

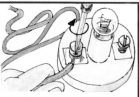

**3.** Fix the end of one wire to the bulb holder.

**4.** Fix the second piece of wire to the other side of the holder.

**5.** Use sticky tape to fix one piece of wire to each end of the battery.

**6.** Watch the bulb light up when the electricity passes through it.

Electricity which moves along a wire is called electric current.

If the current cannot go along its path, or circuit, the light goes off.

# How a telephone works

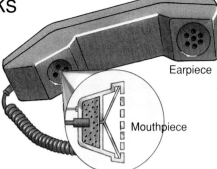

Earpiece

Mouthpiece

When you dial a number, an electric message goes to the telephone exchange. It tells the machine in the exchange which telephone to ring.

There is a microphone inside the mouthpiece. It changes the sound of your voice into electric signals which can be sent along cables.

Some cables go under the sea to take messages to other countries.

The person you are talking to hears you through the earpiece.

Some cables go overground but most go underground. The signals can travel great distances.

There is a tiny loudspeaker inside the earpiece. It changes the signals back into the sound of your voice.

*Internet link* For a link to a website where you can see what's inside a telephone and how it works, go to *www.usborne-quicklinks.com*

# About television

*Internet link* For a link to a website about TVs, go to **www.usborne-quicklinks.com**

Electricity makes your television work as soon as you switch on.

It brings you the pictures you see and the sounds you hear.

## How it works

A television camera turns pictures into electric signals.

The microphone picks up sounds and turns them into more signals.

The signals travel along a cable to a television transmitter.

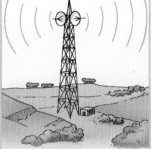

It sends the picture and sound signals through the air.

The television aerial on your house picks up the signals.

The television turns the signals back into pictures and sounds.

## Did you know?

In space, machines called satellites can pick up electrical signals from radios, telephones and televisions. They send them around the world.

The signals are sent by a big transmitter.

# Electricity to your home

Electricity is made in a power station. At the power station it is fed into a transformer.

The transformer makes the electricity stronger so lots of power can be sent to people who need it.

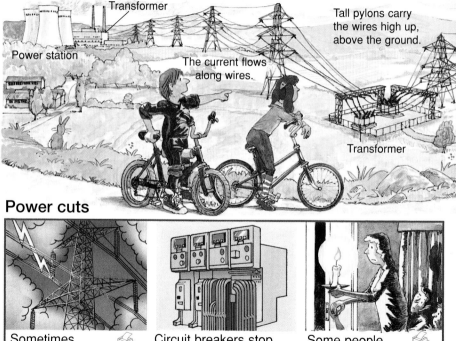

Transformer

Power station

Tall pylons carry the wires high up, above the ground.

The current flows along wires.

Transformer

## Power cuts

Sometimes, lightning strikes a power line and damages it.

Circuit breakers stop electricity flowing along the broken part.

Some people have no electricity until the line is mended.

*Internet link For a link to a website with lots of fun online activities about electricity in our homes and how circuits work, go to www.usborne-quicklinks.com*

Electricity is fed around the country to other transformers. They make it weaker, so you can use it at home.

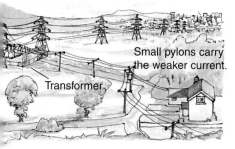

Small pylons carry the weaker current.

Transformer.

## Under the ground

In town, electric cables go under the ground. They bring the current into your home.

Workmen often dig up the road to repair the cables underneath.

## In the house

The wires that carry power round your house are hidden safely in walls, in ceilings or under floors.

## Plugging in

Electricity makes tools, lamps and electrical machines work anywhere you can plug them in.

The plug fits into a socket at the wall. When it is switched on, the electricity goes along the wire.

# How electricity is made

The electricity which is used in your home is made in different kinds of power stations.

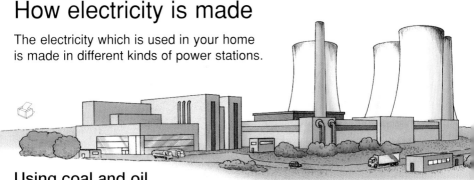

## Using coal and oil

**1.** Coal and oil were made millions of years ago, deep inside the Earth. They are used in some power stations to make electricity.

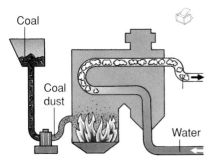

**2.** Coal or oil is burned in a boiler to heat water. When the water gets very hot, it turns into steam.

**3.** The steam goes along pipes to a machine called a turbine. It pushes against the metal blades and makes them spin very fast.

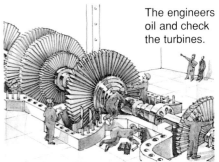

The engineers oil and check the turbines.

**4.** As the turbine spins, it works a machine called a generator. This makes the electricity.

*Internet link* For a link to a website where you can take a virtual tour of a power plant, go to **www.usborne-quicklinks.com**

# Nuclear power stations

Nuclear power stations use fuel called uranium. It is dug out of the ground and used in a special way to make electricity.

## The reactor

The uranium is made into rods. Inside the power station, they are put into the reactor. They are used to make heat.

Visitors can stand behind a window to look at the refuelling machine.

Uranium sends out something dangerous which you cannot see, called radiation. A concrete shield around the reactor keeps it safe.

## Water and steam

The heat made in the reactor boils water in pipes. This turns into steam which goes to the turbines.

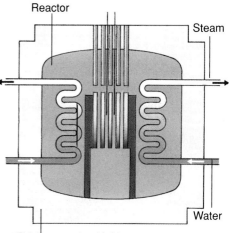

Reactor

Steam

Thick concrete shield

Water

The steam spins the turbines. They work the generator, which makes electricity like generators in other power stations.

*Internet link* For a link to a website where you can watch an animation that explains nuclear power in a simple and fun way, go to **www.usborne-quicklinks.com**

# Power from water

A hydro-electric power station uses falling water to make electricity. The water comes from a huge lake called a reservoir.

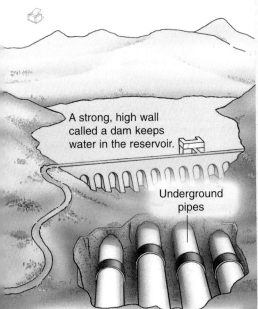

A strong, high wall called a dam keeps water in the reservoir.

Underground pipes

The water from the reservoir rushes downhill, through huge pipelines. Some are 10 metres (33ft) wide.

## The turbines

At the bottom of each pipeline the water works the turbine runner.

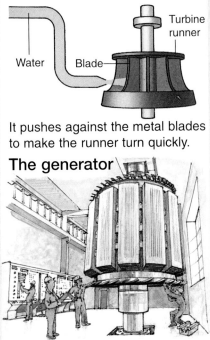

Turbine runner

Water    Blade

It pushes against the metal blades to make the runner turn quickly.

## The generator

When the turbine runner spins, it works the generator and this makes the electricity.

# Saving the water

Top reservoir

Streams or rivers flow into the reservoir all the time and keep it full of water.

In hydro-electric power stations, the water flows away after it has been used to make electricity.

Lower reservoir

Some power stations save the water and use it again and again.

The water works the turbines, then it runs into a lower reservoir.

## The pump

Electricity works huge pumps. They push the water back up to the top reservoir, ready to be used again.

## Fishing

The water which has been used in the power station is clean. Fish can live in the reservoir.

*Internet link* For a link to a website where you can take a look around a hydro-electric power station and click on different parts to find out how they work, go to **www.usborne-quicklinks.com**

# Going places

Electricity is used to work high-speed trains, underground trains, ships and aeroplanes. It even works the controls of space rockets.

## Electric trains

Electric trains get electricity from overhead wires, or a third rail on the ground. It goes into motors which turn the wheels.

Overhead wires

This Japanese "bullet" train can travel up to 443 kilometres (227 miles) an hour.

## Tracks and wires

Trolleybuses pick up electric current from overhead wires.

Some trams pick it up from an electric rail in a slot in the ground.

Underground trains are worked by electricity from extra rails.

*Internet link* For a link to a website with cutaway diagrams of trains including a train that uses electricity, go to **www.usborne-quicklinks.com**

## On the sea and in the air

Electricity works special controls and instruments on ships and aeroplanes.

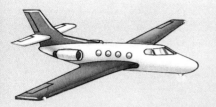

Electric circuits work dials and levers in an aeroplane.

A ship needs electricity to give light and heat. It is also used to work the radio and control the steering.

## Space travel

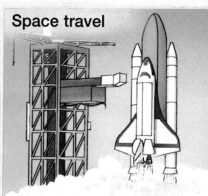

This space shuttle is fired into space by electric signals.

Electric circuits in a computer help the crew to fly the shuttle and work scientific instruments.

*Internet link* For a link to a website where you can launch a space shuttle in an online simulation, go to **www.usborne-quicklinks.com**

17

# Other electricity

There is a kind of electricity called static electricity. It does not flow through wires like electric current, but it does some amazing things.

## Try this

Rub a plastic pen on a woollen jumper for about 30 seconds.

Hold the pen very close to some small pieces of thin paper.

Watch the pieces of paper move towards the pen and stick to it.

## Why it works

This works because static electricity builds up in the pen when you rub it against the wool.

It is the static electricity which pulls the paper towards the pen, making it jump, like magic.

*Internet link* For a link to a website where you can try different ways of making static electricity with experiments to do at home, go to **www.usborne-quicklinks.com**

## Did you know?

Before a thunderstorm, static electricity builds up in storm clouds. When there is too much, it escapes as a flash of lightning.

Conductor

Tall buildings have a metal strip down the outside, called a lightning conductor.

If lightning strikes a building which has a conductor, it travels through the metal, down to the ground.

## Tiny sparks

Lightning hit a tree during a storm in South Dakota, America.

Static electricity made the tree light up. Sparks twinkled on the end of each twig, like fairy lights.

## Electricity in fish

Electric eels can make electricity in their bodies.

They stun their prey with electric shocks before eating it.

*Internet link* For a link to a website with an animation about lightning and static, go to **www.usborne-quicklinks.com**

# More power

One day all the coal and oil which help make electrical power will be used up. Scientists have found other ways of making electricity.

## Using the sun

Something called a solar panel can be put into your roof. It traps the sun's heat to warm the house.

Sunlight can make electricity using a device called a solar cell.

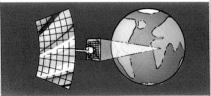

One day, scientists may put a solar collector, made of lots of solar cells, into space. The electricity made would be beamed to Earth.

## Using the wind

The wind has powered windmills for hundreds of years. Now it is used to work special windmills which make electric power.

When the wind blows, it pushes against the huge blades and makes them turn. The moving blades work the generator to make electricity.

*Internet link* For a link to a website where you can watch a video about a teenager who lives in a solar house and find out how solar energy works, go to **www.usborne-quicklinks.com**

## Using the waves

Scientists have worked out how to get power from the movement of waves, far out at sea. It makes electricity to use on land.

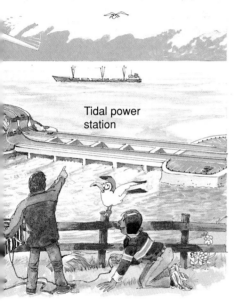

Tidal power station

Some countries have built tidal power stations. These make electricity using the flow of the tide, as it goes in and out.

### High-speed travel

Some electric trains do not need wheels. They hover above special electric tracks.

They speed along at over 400 kilometres (240 miles) an hour.

### Electric cars

Scientists have built cars which run on electricity. But they need to work out many problems before all cars will run without petrol.

# Useful words

You'll find all these words in this book.

## aerial

This picks up electrical signals from the air. If you have a television in your house, or a radio in your car, you need an aerial.

## battery

This has special chemicals inside. They work together to make small amounts of electricity.

## cables

These wires carry electric signals under the ground. They have a special covering to protect them.

## circuit

This is a path of wires. Electricity must travel all the way round to work something electrical.

## filament

This is the very thin coil of wire inside a light bulb. When electricity flows through, it glows brightly.

## generator

This machine makes electricity. Huge generators make electricity in power stations.

## pylons

These are strong, steel towers which carry electric wires safely, high above the ground.

## reactor

This is the part of a nuclear power station where special fuel rods are used to make heat.

## telephone exchange

This is where machines ring the telephone number you have dialled.

## transformer

This changes the electricity to make it stronger or weaker.

## turbine

This is a kind of machine which is worked by water, steam or air, pushing against the blades.

# Internet links

For links to more websites about electricity, go to the Usborne Quicklinks Website at **www.usborne-quicklinks.com** and click on the number of the website you want to visit.

**Website 1** – Here you'll find all kinds of information about energy and electricity, along with stories, puzzles and games. There's a super scientist gallery of energy pioneers, and ideas for your own energy experiments.

**Website 2** – Online activities about energy use in buildings and the environment.

**Website 3** – A fun look at electricity and the different ways it can be generated.

**Website 4** – Try some online activities that will show you how to use electricity safely, both inside and outside your home.

**Website 5** – Travel back in time through the history of electricity using a clickable timeline.

**Website 6** – Listen to thunder and find photos and information about different types of lightning.

**Website 7** – A fun interactive site about things that use electricity in our homes and how to use electricity safely.

**Website 8** – Louie the Lightning Bug explains all about electricity. You can find out what makes an electric eel electric, how our bodies use electricity, and how you can conserve energy and make your house energy efficient.

# Index

battery, 6, 7, 22
cables (electric), 8-12, 22
car, 6, 22
  electric, 21
circuit (electric) 9, 17, 22
current
  electric, 7, 10, 11, 16,
  18

electric, circuit, 7, 17, 22
  cooker, 5
  current, 7, 10, 11, 16,
  18
  eel 19
  generator, 12-14, 20,
  22
  heater, 5
  light bulb, 4, 6, 7, 22
  motor, 16
  shock, 19
  signal, 8, 9, 17, 22
  train, 2, 16, 21
  wires, 4-7, 10, 11, 16,
  22
electrical signal, 9, 22
electricity
  from sunlight, 20

from water, 14, 15
from waves, 21
from wind, 20
static, 18, 19

generator, 12-14, 20, 22

heat (made by electricity),
  2, 4, 5, 17

light, 2, 4, 6, 7, 17
  bulb, 4, 6, 7, 22
lightning, 10, 19
  conductor, 19

motor (electric) 16

plug, 11
power (electrical), 2
  cuts, 10
  line, 10
power station, 10, 12, 20,
  22
  hydro-electric, 14, 15
  nuclear, 13, 22
  tidal, 21
pylon, 10, 11, 22

radiation, 13
radio, 9, 17, 22
reactor, 13, 22

satellites, 9
socket, 11
space shuttle, 17
static electricity, 18, 19
switch (electric), 4

telephone, 8, 9
  exchange, 8, 22
television, 9, 22
  antenna, 9, 22
  camera, 9
  transmitter, 9
train
  electric, 2, 16, 21
  underground, 16
transformer, 10, 11, 22
turbine, 12, 13, 14, 15,
  22

wires
  electric, 4-7, 10, 11, 16,
  22
  heating, 5

First published in 2001 by Usborne Publishing Ltd., Usborne House, 83-85 Saffron Hill, London EC1N 8RT, England. www.usborne.co
Copyright © 2001, 1989 Usborne Publishing Ltd. The name Usborne and the devices ♀ ⛾ are Trade Marks of Usborne Publishing
Ltd. All rights reserved. No part of this publication may be reproduced, stored in a retrieval system, or transmitted in any form or by
any means, electronic, mechanical, photocopying, recording, or otherwise, without the prior permission of the publisher.
Printed in China.